Healing Anger And Depression

Healing Anger, Volume 2

William DeFoore

Published by Halcyon Life Enterprises, LLP, 2023.

HEALING ANGER AND DEPRESSION

First edition. May 29, 2023.

ISBN: 979-8223958048

Written by William DeFoore.

Table of Contents

Healing Anger And Depression

Removing Barriers To Health And Happiness

William G. DeFoore, Ph.D.

Introduction

Health and happiness are naturally occurring, ongoing processes that are inherent to our existence. So why aren't more of us healthy and happy more of the time? It's because of the barriers that block and interfere with that naturally occurring well-being that is our birth right. In this book, you will learn to remove those barriers so that you can live the happy, healthy life that is meant for you.

Emotion is one of the most misunderstood aspects of our human existence. As a result of reading this book, you're going to have a little more understanding of this mysterious realm we call emotion.

We all experience a four-part process when it comes to our emotions. It begins with some kind of oppression from the environment (which happens in some form to all of us), and leads to some kind of suppression, which can result in depression, and leads inevitably to some form of expression. The four-part process is thus oppression, suppression, depression, and expression.

Oppression

THERE ARE DIFFERENT kinds of oppression that all of us are exposed to, and other forms of oppression that are less common. The most common forms of oppression we experience when it comes to our emotions are misinformation and the absence of information.

Every culture has its own version of this. In western culture, we got a type of unintentional, unconscious emotional education, and we all learned these lessons very well. And just to prove to you how well you learned in your emotional education, I'm going to give you a two-part test. The first question is, "How are you doing?" The socially acceptable answer is "Fine." Second question is, "What's wrong?" The socially acceptable answer is "Nothing." "I'm fine, nothing's wrong." That's all you need to know about emotions. Now that is sort of what we've learned, isn't it? It makes sense to say this if it's someone you don't know well, but if you're in conversation with your spouse, close friend or therapist, it doesn't make so much sense.

So that's the misinformation. The misinformation is, you're supposed to be fine with nothing wrong all of the time. And if you decide you want to tell someone how you really feel, you need some type of vocabulary for talking about your emotions, which leads us to the next most common form of oppression – the absence of information.

The absence of information is demonstrated when we look at how most schools approach the topic of emotion, emotional health, and communicating emotions in relationships. Anybody remember studying that? Did you have any classes on how to build and maintain joyful, loving relationships?

We got our math and our science and our English. Those are important, right? But why haven't we made a study of this powerful thing that we call human emotion that determines the success of our parenting relationships, marriages, friendships, and even affects the ups and downs of the stock market? Many progressive schools are beginning to teach emotional and social intelligence skills, but most of us grew up with little or no guidance about emotions, even from our families, churches, and other community organizations.

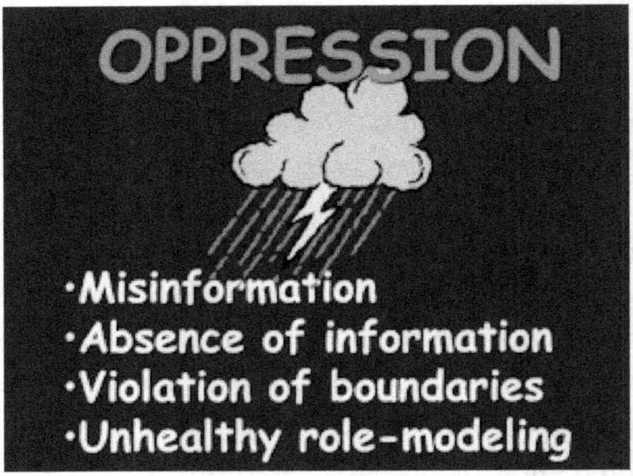

ANOTHER FORM OF OPPRESSION that happened to all of us in one way or another is a violation of boundaries. Now, that sounds like an extreme thing, but who didn't get some kind of bullying or unkindness at school, or among siblings or peers? Who didn't have a parent, teacher, or caregiver that got a little short tempered one day and said, "Shut up!" or called us names, or maybe hit us a little too hard. It happens, doesn't it? This is what it means to be a human being raised by humans.

Some of us had our boundaries violated in very extreme ways, such as physical abuse, sexual abuse, or maybe a lot of extended verbal and emotional abuse. These are powerful forms of oppression, with significant ramifications.

And we all had some experience with unhealthy role modelling, because we were raised by imperfect human beings, however wonderful our parents and caregivers may have been in some ways. They weren't always giving the perfect example of how to deal with emotions. Maybe they held their anger in too long before it came out one way or the other, or maybe they just held it in all the time and became depressed.

Maybe they were consumed with fear, and they had panic and anxiety and transferred some of that to us. They may have had some kind of compulsive/addictive disorder that prevented a healthy emotional relationship. You can see how we were all affected by these types of influences from our environment.

Suppression

THIS LEADS TO THE NEXT phase in our emotional process, most commonly known as suppression.

Because we weren't taught and guided, we learned (unconsciously) to suppress our emotions from early in life. After suppressing your emotions for some time, you start to develop a sort of disconnect from your body. It just starts to not feel so good down there in your gut, chest, and other regions because of all this chronic body tension. So there will be some inevitable aches and pains, digestive problems, and respiratory problems.

So, if you're going to continue to say "I'm fine, nothing's wrong," then you're going to have to start living from the neck up. You're going to have to pretend that stuff that's going on down there is not happening. When it comes to our body awareness and emotional self-awareness, we have learned to lie to ourselves and to each other.

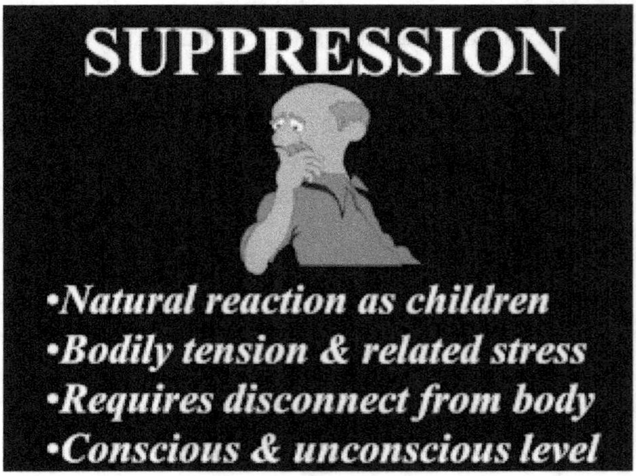
SUPPRESSION
•Natural reaction as children
•Bodily tension & related stress
•Requires disconnect from body
•Conscious & unconscious level

A CLASSIC SCENARIO is the gentleman who says, "I'm fine, nothing's wrong. It's a great day," while ignoring what is going on in his body and emotions, then boom, heart attack. This gentleman was real familiar with that burning pain in his chest, because it had been there for a long time. He was taking medication for it. He got to the point where he could pretend everything was fine, even while his chest was burning.

Now we're talking about physical symptoms and heart trouble, in the same context with suppressing emotions. That is because suppressing emotions leads to hypertension, depression, and anxiety, all of which deplete the immune system and increase the likelihood of malady (Pietrangelo 2019).

So this is what we learned to do with chronically held tension. And it's totally unconscious. If something happens that upsets you, you don't have to decide whether to burst into tears or just hold onto those emotions. You don't have to think about it, do you?

You can't hold an emotion in your body without tensing your muscles. You cannot be totally physically relaxed, breathing deep into your diaphragm and holding onto your emotions at the same time. So, relaxation is a key component of expressing and releasing emotion.

Let's say something scary happens. Maybe you read a news report about a stock that you're holding and the possibility that the bottom might fall out of it. Or you find out about some type of health problem that affects you or a loved one. Do we have to decide whether to scream or not? No. You just automatically pretend that everything's okay. And that's not all bad. It can actually be a good thing. It is healthy to express emotions in the right place and at the right time, and unhealthy to express them in inappropriate contexts.

And it is unhealthy to keep them inside and never express them at all.

We're going through the four-part process of oppression, suppression, depression, and expression. Now let's look at this baffling issue of depression, particularly the type of depression that most of us deal with on a fairly regular basis.

Chapter One: Understanding Depression

The kind of depression that we're focusing on is the kind that all of us deal with to some extent. I'm not really talking about the kind of clinical depression that is debilitating, where a person can't get out of bed. To give you an idea of this, I want to ask you just to think through something with me for a moment.

When you go through your everyday life and you're in traffic, or in a place of business, and you glance at the other people's faces and eyes, how often do you see expressions of joy, radiance, love, or peace? A lot, or a little? Probably not very often. As a matter of fact, when we do see that, we think there's something not quite right about that person. You just can't be that happy in this world.

By contrast, how often do we see looks of anxiety, discontent, or boredom? How often do we see serious looks, concerned looks, perhaps unfriendly looks. That's what we consider to be normal, isn't it? We only consider it to be normal because it is what the norm is doing.

I've often had clients say to me, usually early on in the counseling process, "I just want to be normal." And I say, "Well, you are already normal, mission accomplished. What else do you want to do?" Normal is somewhere between the extremes of whatever group you're a part of. If you're in a group, family, city, or country with a lot of anger and frustration, then angry and frustrated are normal. If you're fortunate enough to be in a group that is happy and loving, then happy and loving are normal.

So what's a better focus than normal? Let's talk about what it means to be emotionally healthy. To be emotionally healthy means that most of the time, you feel joyful, peaceful, and loving. Excellent emotional health is unfortunately about as rare as excellent physical health.

I'm not saying that to be healthy means to never get sick or have anything wrong, but I believe that our average state of physical and emotional health is way below where it could be, and where it needs to be.

So, this kind of depression is what we have decided is normal, and yet it's not healthy and it's not where we want to be if we want to live a long and vibrant life. One way of understanding depression is as unexpressed pain, fear and anger. These are the three big negative emotions that we never learned about in school, and not a day goes by in most of our lives where we don't feel one of those emotions. And most days we feel all of them, off and on throughout the day. Some people, whether they know it or not, even live in constant fear. Others are always angry and many people are just plain sad all of the time. Again, that's kind of normal, so we don't even think about it that much.

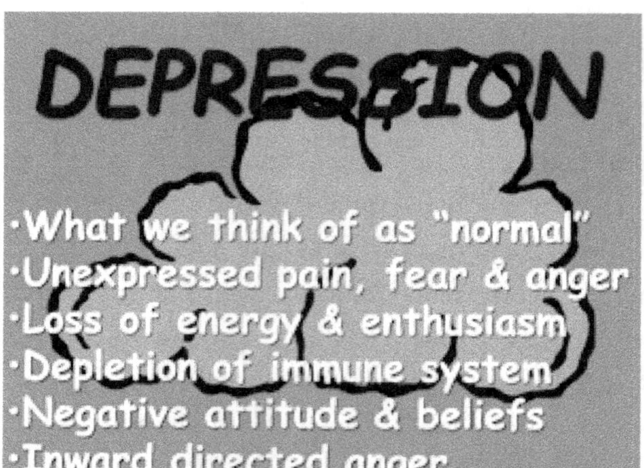

HOLDING THESE EMOTIONS inside requires exerting some pressure within your body/mind system. When you chronically depress or suppress your emotions, you become depressed. So depression is the holding of negative emotions.

In this situation, you don't feel them, release them, and move on. You just feel them, and hold them, and then you feel them more and more, and the internal burden gets heavier and heavier. That's why people who are depressed feel a heaviness, a density, or a sluggishness inside. Inevitably with this there's going to be a loss of energy and enthusiasm.

If I could give you a bottle of pills, all natural ingredients, no side effects, that would raise your level of energy and enthusiasm throughout the day every day, would anybody be interested? Of course. We all want more of that, don't we?

This depression that we consider to be normal depletes our energy and enthusiasm, to the point that some people feel they don't have any energy at all. The heaviness is sometimes so great that you may feel like you can barely lift your foot to get it in front of the other one.

Medical science has long ago established and continues to prove that when we're depressed, our immune system functions less effectively. Which means what? It means that you're likely to get sick if you stay depressed for too long. The less effectively your immune system functions, the longer it takes to recover when you are sick and the more likely you are to get sick.

Think of all the contagious diseases there are floating around out there all the time. Now, why do some people get them, and some people don't? Or why do you get it one time and you don't at another time? As far as we know, it's because of the immune system. When your immune system is working well, you can ward off highly contagious, dangerous disease. And when the immune system is not functioning well, one little cold germ and boom! You're out for a week.

We're making a connection here between how we deal with our emotions, the condition of depression, and depletion of the immune system.

Inevitably, the mind is going to go negative in this process. It's not possible to have a depressed feeling, no energy or enthusiasm, and very positive thoughts. And the negative thoughts lead to a negative attitude, and will feed into old negative, self-defeating beliefs. Changing your thoughts can actually help sometimes, but there's more to healing depression than that. We'll go further into the healing process later.

Another way of understanding depression is to see it as a result of inward directed anger. Thinking, "All of these problems are because of me. It's my fault." While it is important to take responsibility, you just cannot afford to go completely negative toward yourself and expect to heal.

Think of it like this. The angry person is putting the blame outside, putting the responsibility and power on others. The depressed person is putting the blame inside, and yet feeling powerless to make the necessary changes.

Chapter Two: Healthy And Unhealthy Emotional Expression

Now for the fourth part of the oppression, suppression, depression, expression process. To understand what we mean by emotional expression, let's start with the idea of emotion as e-motion, or energy in motion. Emotion is meant to move. When it doesn't move, it becomes stagnant and interferes with the natural functioning of your body and mind.

When you have an emotion such as fear, sorrow, anger, or even joy or love and you don't do anything to express it, that means you're holding it inside, tensing both small and complex muscle groups in your body in the process. This muscle tension, particularly when it's chronic, will interfere with your circulation, respiration, and digestion.

Clearly, we need to find some way to move, release, and express these emotions so that they don't interfere with our health. So now let's talk about different forms of emotional expression.

We know all about unhealthy emotional expression, right? Particularly when it comes to anger. You can probably give a lot of examples of unhealthy expression of anger. Yelling, throwing things, passive-aggressive behavior, and outright violence come to mind.

By contrast, how many examples of healthy anger expression can you think of? Much fewer, I'm sure.

So far in this chapter, we've established that your emotions need to be moved, released, and expressed. But I'm sure you understand that this needs to happen in ways that do no harm to you or others, or else we've just replaced one problem with another.

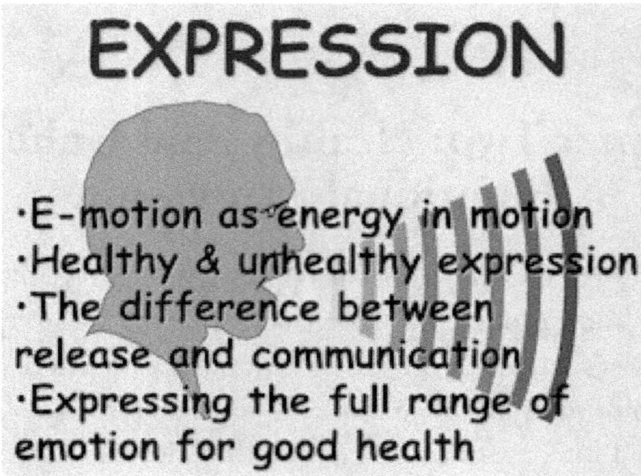

NOW, IN ORDER TO UNDERSTAND healthy and unhealthy emotional expression, we've really got to look at the difference between release and communication. This is a very important distinction.

I'm going to put this in the context of a story you may be able to relate to. Let's say that it's time for a family gathering and you have decided that you are going to prepare a special dinner for everyone. Your spouse has agreed to do a few things, not big things, just pick up the turkey that's being cooked elsewhere, as well as ingredients for the dressing and other details like that. And you've got everything timed down to the minute. The guests are arriving at a certain time, and you've made it very clear to your spouse that you need the turkey and ingredients by a certain time.

You've spent an evening doing most of the preparations, and now the day of the gathering has arrived. Your spouse agreed to have everything and be back at the house by 5pm. It's 5:30, and no call. Your calls go straight to voice mail. The guests will start to arrive soon. 6pm comes and goes, still no communication or response to your messages. Now it's 6:30. What feelings are you having? What's going through your mind? First you got angry, then you got worried. Then you got angry again, and back to worry. You're afraid they've been in an accident, and they're injured or dead. And the worry/anger combination means that you're thinking "If they're not dead, I'm going to kill them."

You might even cycle through a more calm feeling, in which you feel sad. You reflect on your years of marriage, and all you've been through together. It hurts your feelings that this person has let you down in this way. Then back to fear and anger.

So, you're kind of on an emotional rollercoaster, right? And let's say that you happen to be somebody who occasionally blows up when you're really angry. Finally, you hear the car pull up in the driveway and you feel relieved that they're not dead. You can see that they're walking toward the house, so you know that they're not seriously injured. You can't wait for that door to open because you want to (multiple choice) 1) release or 2) communicate. Because you're somewhat volatile, you want to release, and you're not even thinking about communicating.

Think about it for a moment. In this situation, are you interested in what they have to say? Not yet. Not particularly. Maybe later, but not particularly. You want to let your volcano explode on them, right? You've been stewing in your own emotional juices, and you need to blow off steam.

Now, let's put yourself on the other side of the situation, because we've all probably been on both sides of this. You're the one who is late and didn't call. Walking up to the door, you know you've messed up. Are you really interested in what your spouse is going to say? Are you thinking, "I wonder what they're going to have to say?"

Is It Release Or Is It Communication?

NO, THOSE ARE MOST likely not your thoughts. You're preparing your defense. You know you're about to get blasted, and this is not going to be about communication. This is going to be battle. This is going to be warfare. No real communication is going to happen.

This is where we get into problems, particularly in intimate relationships. We get release and communication mixed up. When you release built up negative emotion in somebody else's face, or through electronic connections, not only does it not communicate well, it eliminates the possibility of communication. It's an attack.

When you're mad and getting ready to explode, you're not aware that you're about to damage the relationship. You probably think you're going to really get your message across. You might think "I'm going to let him know once and for all just exactly how I feel about this. And he's going to listen to me because I'm going to be screaming at the top of my lungs." I've heard people say, "I have to yell or they won't hear me."

But the thing is, we don't listen to people that are yelling. That kind of verbal aggression just triggers our defense mechanisms, and our listening skills go out the window. So our mind is not engaged to really understand the words being spoken (or yelled, in this case).

So, the point here is, if we can't separate release from communication, then we're going to lose the ability to communicate. How many marriages do you think have communication as an issue? I would guess most of them.

Now let's discuss specifically about how to release emotion in healthy ways, and how to communicate effectively in emotionally tense situations.

It's not hard to communicate when everything's cool. When you're totally relaxed, communication is a breeze. So we're going to focus on how to communicate when there's stress and tension in the air.

To be emotionally healthy, we need to express, release, and communicate the full range of emotion from the deepest sorrow to the greatest joy. Where we get off track is when we express only the anger, only the fear, or only the sorrow. As we'll discuss further when we look at healthy communication tools, we need to express these difficult emotions in the context of our love and appreciation. That makes them more palatable, and increases the likelihood that you will be heard and understood.

When we allow one emotion to take over, it's like a dam burst. People breaking down in tears in public, or screaming at someone are some fairly familiar examples. These types of situations are what gives the term "emotional" a negative meaning.

And because most of us have squeezed ourselves into this thin grey line of "I'm fine, nothing's wrong," we are also a little shocked or embarrassed if we see someone that seems way too happy or far too affectionate. We call this "normal."

What is healthy is to be able to express all of your emotions appropriately, at the right time and place, with the right person, express the full range of emotion.

When we feel sorrow, we need to be able to express that. When we feel anger, fear, we need to be able to express that. We need to be able to express our joy and our love and our creativity. And we need to express these emotions in ways that are healthy. Thinking again of release and communication, releasing is done alone, and of course communication involves another person or other people. The goal is for the release to provide relief, and to do no harm to you or others. And the goal for communication is to express your emotions in such a way that you are heard and understood by others.

That's a big part of healthy emotional expression. We'll give you a lot more detail on that later in the book.

Chapter Three: Anger, Depression, And Your Health

So, as I mentioned, anger is putting the blame outside. Depression puts it inside. Anger is directed at someone or something outside yourself. The finger is pointing at the problem, the cause of our anger, and that is exactly where we're putting our power, even though we don't know it.

You might feel powerful when you're ranting and raving against the injustice, but in fact you're diminishing your power unless your anger is healthy. Anger can actually make you feel strong and righteous, but as long as we see the cause of our problems outside, where is the power, really?

IT'S OUT THERE, ISN'T it? I'm perceiving that the power is out there. The angry person believes that he or she is a victim, and in some cases that is completely understandable. What we're trying to do here is help you move through the anger, and use it to solve your problems instead of getting stuck in it.

Some of the thoughts that go with anger are, "I'm angry because he wouldn't..." "I'm angry because she did that..." "I'm angry because they won't..."

The angry person is putting the power out where the finger is pointing. But you probably heard if there's one finger pointing out that way, there's three pointing back. The responsibility is here with me. I'm the only one that can change how I feel. Now, I can't change what other people are doing, but I can sure change how I feel. That takes you right out of the victim role.

So that blaming game is giving your power away. And when you give your power away, you're going to feel powerless. When I've worked with people who have had serious problems with anger, one of the things that they tell me consistently is right before that big explosion, what they're feeling inside is powerless. Powerlessness is an intolerable feeling to most people, and so the unconscious "solution" is to go to the most primitive, easy-access form of power. That is the "fight" reflex...anger.

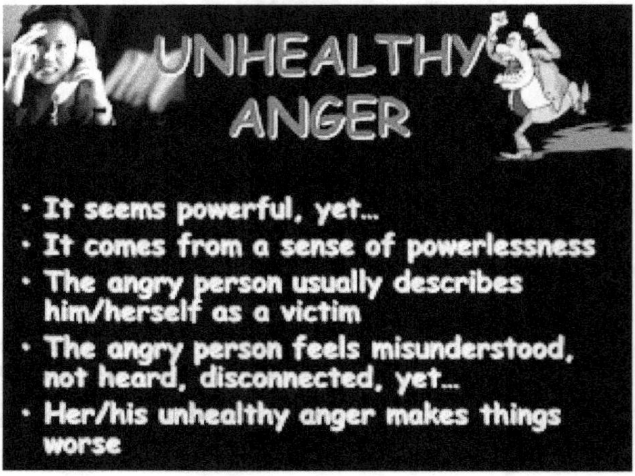

SO, UNHEALTHY ANGER is a primitive way to try to get power. In these situations, the person feels powerless, then goes into anger, and starts to feel pumped up with all of the adrenaline and the false sense of power that comes with it. Because this is an unconscious process, good sense and moral judgment go by the wayside, and so people get hurt.

Then the adrenaline subsides, and good sense returns. We have the clarity to survey the damage and realize what we've said and done, and then we don't feel very powerful. And that's when the guilt sets in and we have to bank the apology, clean up the mess.

How Does Emotion Become Toxic?

HOW DOES SOMETHING as natural as emotion become toxic? It happens in the same way that anything else becomes toxic, through the lack of fluid movement. When we don't express our emotions with healthy release and communication, they stagnate. That's how unexpressed emotions become toxic over time, ultimately blocking the movement of healing energy in the body and healthy communication in relationships.

Have you ever known anybody who had old anger that just keeps simmering, boiling over, and then goes back to simmering? We see that in individuals, but we also see it in countries that have generational conflict. We even see it among families, such as in the instance of family feuds that have lasted up to 30 years.

Old anger is ugly, toxic, and it makes people sick. It sometimes even costs lives. This stagnation and toxifying process applies to other emotions as well. Old unresolved fear turns to nervous tension, panic, and anxiety. Unexpressed sorrow becomes depression, bitterness, and despair.

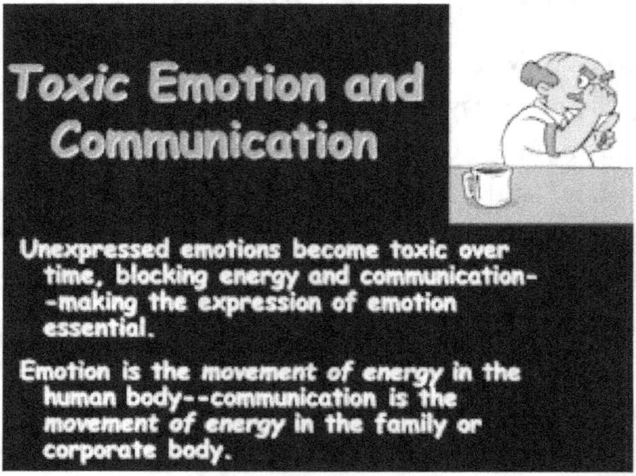

LET'S GO BACK TO THE family gathering scenario for a moment. Let's say I'm the one who's been preparing this special dinner and my spouse is late coming back. Let's imagine that I don't say anything. She comes in and says "Oh, I'm so sorry. This happened and that happened, and I forgot to pick up the groceries, but maybe there's still time if I hurry."

And I say, "That's fine." She says, "Are you mad?" I respond with "No, I'm fine. Nothing's wrong." I just hold all of my emotions inside. What happens to our communication from that point? It comes to a standstill. So, when I suppress my emotion, it blocks communication.

Now it wouldn't do me any more good to scream at her, right? That stops communication too. So, we got to find a third alternative. Suppressing how I feel doesn't work and exploding doesn't work. But those are the two choices that historically we've been stuck with...shouting or pouting. No wonder we've had so much trouble with our emotions and our relationships.

What goes along with the pouting? The anger is still there, isn't it? It just comes out sideways, indirectly. This is called passive-aggressive behavior, which can be damaging in a lot of different ways. The passive-aggressive person usually doesn't consciously know what they're doing, but the effect on the other end is frustration, irritation, and a lot of hurt feelings.

To have healthy relationships, we have to learn to express our emotions with integrity, respect, and compassion.

If emotion is the movement of energy in the human body, then communication is the movement of energy in relationships. Blockage in communication can destroy marriage, families, and organizations.

I was working with a business executive, who used this example to emphasize the importance of communication in his company. He said "You know I get with you guys and I say, okay, this is my plan. I think we ought to go in that direction with this new project. Are you with me?" Everyone agrees, because he's at the head, right? He's the leader.

So, he continues, "I head off in the direction I chose, and the next thing I know I hit a dead end, or I fall off a cliff." Then I hear someone in my company say "I knew that would happen." And the leader asks, "Why didn't somebody tell me? Why go along with a plan that is likely to fail?"

I think you know the most common answer. "You're the boss. I'd probably get my head bit off if I disagreed with your plan."

So why didn't anybody tell him? Fear. Fear of judgment, reprimand, or embarrassment. That's a big communication stopper. In families, why would an adolescent be afraid to talk to mom or dad about a sexual question? Probably get a lecture. It might activate mom or dad's fears or biases. In other words, they would hear a whole lot of stuff they don't want to hear. Why would the angry adolescent not want to tell his mom and dad that he's been thinking about doing violent things at school?

Again, fear. Fear of having to go to the doctor, get put on medication, get yelled at or ignored. Any response other than loving, understanding, listening, support, and genuine help, is going to cause fear, and suppressed fear blocks communication.

In a healthy family where a child is encouraged to talk about their emotions, the son might go to his dad and say, "Dad, I want to talk about some things, but I'm afraid you'll get mad." Clearly, that's a step in the right direction, because at least the child is talking, and not just keeping it inside. A healthy dad would listen, and encourage his son to go ahead and tell him, with the promise that he would try to understand.

How To Stay In Charge Of Your Own Mood

HAVE YOU EVER FOUND yourself brought down by hanging around with certain people? It's like you caught their mood from them. It doesn't have to be like that. You can remain in charge of your mood, and the key is to learn the tools of healthy emotional expression.

An interesting research study showed that when subjects were divided into pairs and given topics to discuss, whoever expressed the strongest emotion tended to pass their mood to the other person. (Sullins 1991). Have you ever been in a situation where somebody is ranting and raving about something or they're real scared and they're telling you all about it? If you're pulled into their story, and don't have a very strong story of your own going, you will take on their mood.

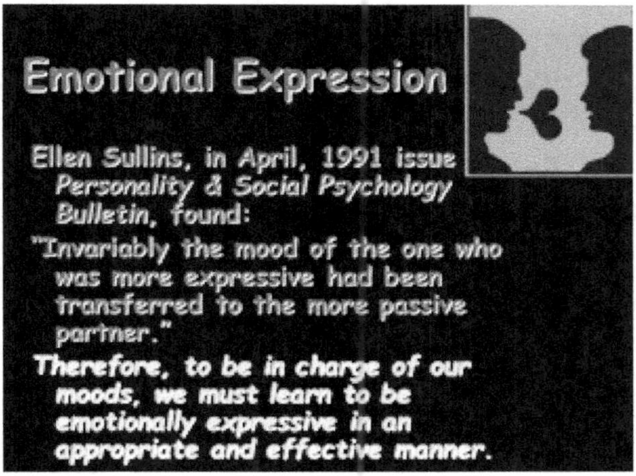

OF COURSE YOU WON'T mind at all if your mood is a little low, and you "catch" the mood of an upbeat, happy person, but it's no fun at all to start your day off happy and then get thrown off by someone who's very vocal with their negativity.

Examples of healthy emotional expression in this scenario would be two-fold. First is your internal process, the healthy emotional expression going on inside your own mind, or the story you're telling yourself. This is the most important part of claiming your mood, because it is totally up to you and does not depend on anyone else.

The second form of healthy emotional expression to maintain your own mood involves the words you speak out loud to the other person. You definitely don't want to get into an argument, trying to prove that you're right and they are wrong. That never really works. What you can say would be something like this: "Ok, I think I get what you're saying, and I can see how it would look that way to you. And I can see why that would be very upsetting. I see things differently." If the person is open to how you see things, then you can elaborate upon your different story.

Many times, however, the very expressive person in the bad mood just wants to vent or rant, and is not really interested in other viewpoints. In those cases, it's best to just move on with your day as quickly as possible, while continuing to keep your internal dialogue on a more positive level.

Chapter Four: The Emotional Education You Never Got

Wouldn't it be great if we had been taught as children how to understand, manage, and express our emotions in healthy ways? It would have helped us in so many ways, and prevented many of the problems we've had.

We're going to look at our basic emotional needs, and then examine how we develop emotionally from infancy to adulthood.

The Need To Love And Be Loved

OUR BASIC EMOTIONAL need as human beings is to love and be loved. We were born with this need, and it is just as strong today as it was the day we were born. The difference is that as infants we were completely dependent on our caregivers for this, and as adults we have a lot more choice in how we address our needs.

We can't address the need to love and be loved without addressing the need for touch. Touch is an irreplaceable part of how love is communicated. As revealed in the research around *Frederick's Experiment* (2023), children deprived of touch fail to thrive, and in many cases do not survive. This was an experiment conducted in the thirteenth century that was inhuman to say the least, but clearly revealed what most of would have known anyway. Children absolutely need touch, as an essential component of feeling loved.

IMAGINE A SITUATION in which a parent is averse to touch, which is unfortunately that all that uncommon. She often tells her child "I love you," but only touches the child in a functional way, as a part of cleaning and clothing the child. The child hears the words of endearment, but does not feel loved, in the absence of gentle, affectionate, and nurturing touch.

And we need touch as adults just as much as we did when we were infants. The difference is that we have learned to adapt, and many people who are actually touch deprived are not actually aware of their unmet need. This can lead to symptoms as diverse as depression and sex addiction.

Many of us as adults are touch deprived and love deprived. We consider it to be "normal." While it may in fact be normal, it is not healthy by any means. Symptoms of touch deprivation include, depression, decreased life satisfaction, fatigue, problems sleeping, and anxiety.

Since touch is an essential part of love, many of us are actually love deprived, without realizing it. As we move through this book, there will be more and more emphasis on the importance of expressing your love, which will increase the likelihood of receiving love. We are moving from the problem to the solution.

Think of the people you love the most in the world. Ask yourself, do they know how much you love them? Some would say yes, some would say no, or I don't know. Expressing the real depths of love that we feel inside is scary, because it's really hard for us to reach all the way down inside and bring that out. And yet, I want to suggest to you that expressing the depths of your love is one of the best things you can do, not only for your relationship, but for your physical health as well. Because that love is the heart of the matter of who you are. It's at the core of your entire life experience.

The Inevitable Experience Of Pain, Sorrow And Fear

NOW, WHERE HAVE WE been the most hurt in our lives? What kind of relationships? Relationships with strangers? No. We have been hurt the most by some of those who were closest to us, not because they were necessarily bad, but because that is where we are the most vulnerable. Think about it...in what relationship have we been the most vulnerable emotionally and physically? Our relationships with our parents, primary caregivers, and other significant loved ones. As infants, our hearts and minds are wide open. We are defenseless, and we absorb whatever comes, just like a sponge soaks up water. There is no more vulnerable condition for human beings than that.

AS ADULTS, WE HAVE all kinds of defense mechanisms, but as infants we had no protection whatsoever. As adults, we can pretend and even believe "I'm fine, nothing's wrong," while we are being attacked or ignored, but as infants, whatever happens goes right in.

Since childhood is the most vulnerable time of our lives, that's where we experienced the deepest pain and sorrow. Much of that happened before we were even fully conscious, so many of the memories are unconscious for us today.

To get a feel for this, ask yourself, what was your earliest worst experience. Most people have pretty easy access to those memories. Generally, it's around the age of three to seven years of age. That's where most people have that earliest worst memory, although some are earlier and some are later.

The reason your mind remembers that experience, and has forgotten all of other memories is not because you're getting old and losing your memory. It's because that one memory is important and the others are not, as reported in the research showing the impact of emotion on memory (Kenginger 2009). By important, I mean it has value for you in terms of your self-awareness and personal growth. Those easily recalled memories are storehouses for significant information about your emotional life.

In addition to your earliest worst memory, you probably can also recall what you would consider to be your earliest best memory. What about the relationships where you felt the most acknowledged and loved? You probably also remember those.

These strong feelings of love, joy, and sorrow are held deep inside. There is tremendous energy stored there, and that energy needs to move. In other words, those stories need to be told. If we leave those powerful emotional memories locked away, they will not only block our energy, they will interfere with our ability to give and receive love.

Unexpressed pain and sorrow block our access to love. Couples who experience significant loss, for example, and do not communicate about their sorrow are going to have trouble. In some cases, the relationship might even end.

We don't express our pain and sorrow because it's fun, or because we look good while we're doing it. We express pain and sorrow because if we don't, it blocks our capacity for love and joy.

HOWEVER WE WERE THE most hurt, that is where we will have the greatest fear. If we were hurt by abandonment, the death of a parent at an early age, or by some kind of violation, our fears as adults are going to be around those same kinds of possibilities in our lives.

The occurrence of fear as a part of our emotional development is as natural as learning to walk and talk. Yet we received little or no guidance for our emotional development, and a lot of focus on our physical performance.

The Protective Function Of Anger

SO FAR IN OUR EMOTIONAL development we have looked at three stages; the need to love and be loved, the experience of pain and sorrow, and the resulting development of fear. These are a highly vulnerable stages, so we need some kind of protection in this world. This is where the emotion of anger comes in. Anger is the protective emotion.

Anger usually starts showing up around 18-24 months. That's where the child starts feeling a little bit of her power, and pushes back against things she doesn't want. She might scream to avoid that bath, or throw that bowl of creamed carrots on the floor because she doesn't want to eat it, or just because she's feeling a little cantankerous.

So that energy of anger starts coming out naturally, in different ways and at different times for all of us. When your anger showed up, was it well received? Probably not. Most of us had our anger punished or ignored.

So, what did you learn about your anger growing up? You probably learned that nothing will be accomplished with it, it does you no good. Or you may have learned that you might get hurt if you show it. So, suppression is the natural choice, right? Hold your anger inside. Some of us held it inside until we exploded. Some of us just held it inside until it made us sick, but either way, suppressing anger never turns out well.

On the contrary, some of us might have been rewarded for our anger. We might have learned that if we threw a tantrum, we would get our way. This is just as damaging as getting punished or ignored, because it teaches you that anger is a good way to control your environment and push people into what you want them to do. This can sometimes lead to anger addiction, where a person is caught in an unconscious loop of resorting to destructive anger over and over, doing more damage all of the time.

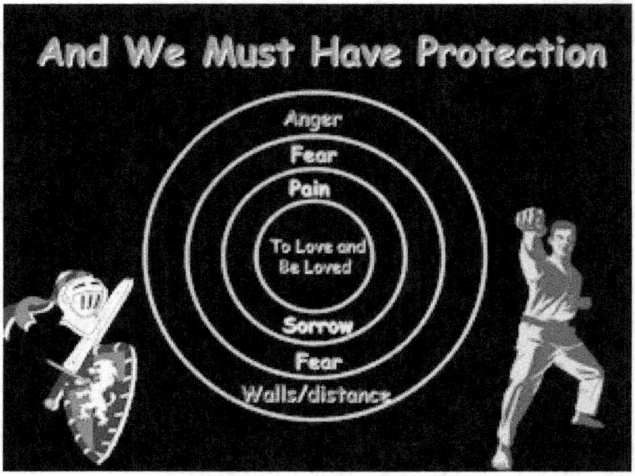

Creating Walls And Distance For Protection

AS WE LEARN THAT ANGER is not working that well, we turn to another form of protection that is tied in with anger suppression. We learned to put up walls, and create distance from others in multiple ways.

You can see the fight or flight reflex in these choices for protection. Anger is the fight reaction, and the walls and distance are for the purpose of flight, a means of somehow escaping the threat or pain. So, you either stand up and speak out against the problem, or you find a way to exit.

The problem with option two is that you can't always leave. As children, we aren't likely to pack up our little bag of toys and go toddling out the front door looking for better parents. So, what kind of flight or withdrawal do we choose when we can't physically leave the situation?

We choose some type of internal withdrawal or shut down. We learn to be quiet, to be good little boys and girls. We withdraw and pull into our shell in order to avoid being rejected or punished, and in order to get love. This is a very natural process.

But as you can see in these concentric circles, moving from the inside out to the edges, we're sort of going through a pretty difficult process here. And all of this is happening before we're even aware of what's going on, so it's primarily unconscious. That's why we're talking about these processes now, so that you can be more consciously aware and able to make choices.

The Development Of The Performer

THEN PRETTY SOON WE have to learn how to give the world what it wants, which is none of this stuff, none of the pain, fear, and anger. We've got to learn how to perform and pretend that everything's okay, even when it's not. This is where we learn how to say, "I'm fine. Nothing's wrong".

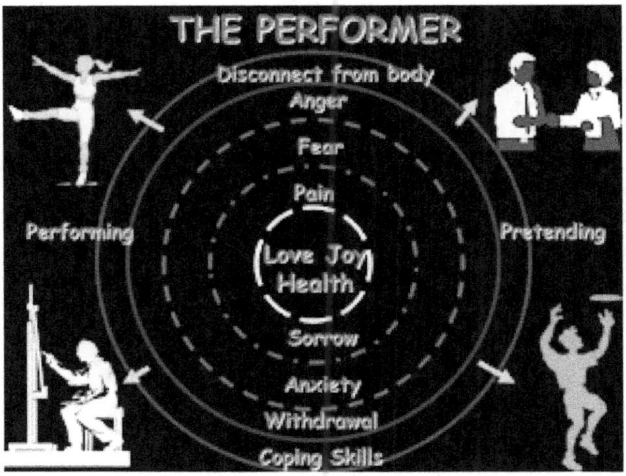

WE LEARN HOW TO COPE with the world that doesn't really understand or want to deal with our pain and fear and anger. We learn how to adapt to what the world wants and doesn't want. In order to do that, you've got to disconnect from your body, because all of those inner emotions of pain, fear, and anger are residing in your heart and in your gut.

This is why a lot of people have a slumped posture. The curved back is like the tortoise shell curving around the vulnerable front middle region of the heart and the gut. This closing and contracting process reduces blood flow to those vital functions such as respiration and digestion, thereby increasing the likelihood of illness over time.

In a way, the performer can also be a pretender, pretending that everything is fine when it's not. Pretending that you don't need to love and be loved, that you are not vulnerable at your core. Pretending that you don't have all of those unacceptable emotions until your system starts to falter, and you can't pretend anymore. The pretending and disconnected performance only work so long before they just don't work so well any more. This is because the energy source you need in order to function well on an ongoing basis through your life is right there at the core of your being.

When you cut yourself off from your core with denying and pretending, you cut yourself off from your energy source, the very life force that animates and enlivens all that you are.

That's why we need to make the inner journey, to remove the barriers to your naturally life-giving source of energy and well-being.

Chapter Five: The Irreplaceable Inner Journey

All of our lives, we have been educated about and directed toward the outer realms of our existence. Serve others, impress others, win others' approval. Do well, perform well, get the grade, make the money, win the love of that special person. So our initial journey in life is an outer one, and the inner journey only begins when we find that our performance in the outer journey is beginning to falter.

Keep in mind, however, that the inner journey is still optional. Many people choose to deal with the performance disruptions with medication, drug and alcohol addiction, and outright, ongoing denial. Sadly, these patterns lead to great hardship and suffering.

Here's where we get to the real and lasting solution to the problem. We have to learn to take responsibility for ourselves. We have to learn to have an internal focus and to explore those uncharted realms of anger, fear, pain, and our incredibly strong need to love and be loved.

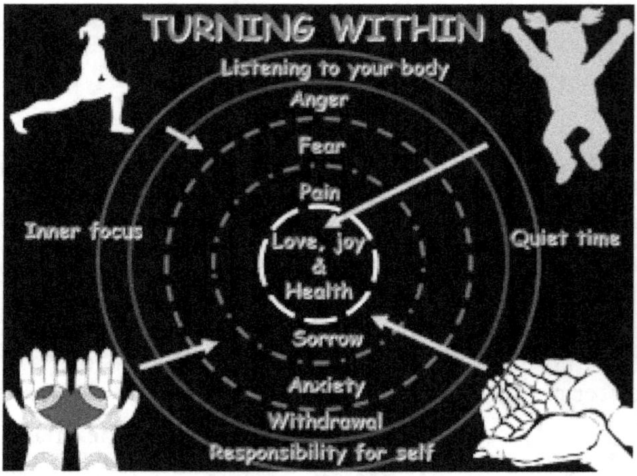

AS YOU BEGIN LOOKING within yourself for solutions rather than focusing exclusively outside yourself, you will also need to begin listening to your body. Your body has wisdom that your mind knows nothing about. And to begin accessing that wisdom, you must also begin taking quiet time for reflection and self-awareness.

When I talk about listening to your body, I am also talking about listening to your emotions. Your body and your emotions are not actually separate. If you're frequently anxious, your breathing will be shallow and your muscles will be tense. If you're too easily angered, your chest and shoulders might be tight a lot of the time. Emotion lives in your body.

A physician named Jerome Groopman wrote a book called *Second Opinions*, in which he said that ideally, physicians would spend a minimum of 30 minutes with each of their patients (2001). This is not the norm, as you know.

He suggests a minimum of 30 minutes with each patient in order for the physician to learn as much as possible about what patient has thought, felt, or imagined about what's going on in their body. It would also give him a chance to learn of significant life events and changes that may impact the patient's health.

What he was saying is that the patient's knowledge and intuitive sense of what's going on is highly valuable information for a physician in coming up with the right treatment. Yet how many physicians have the luxury or take the time to gather that kind of information? And how many of us respect our own intuition and our own knowledge of our bodies, enough to share it if it were asked for.

Your Inner Physician

WE KNOW THAT HEALING comes from within the body, and the very best that medical science can provide is treatment to facilitate that internal healing process. Cellular biologist Bruce Lipton has found in his research that human cells contain the blueprint for healing and well-being we need to be whole and healthy (Lipton 2016). All medical treatment, such as medications and surgical procedures are designed to remove barriers to the body's natural internal healing processes.

I want to suggest to you that your body/mind complex is brilliant far beyond anything that you've ever imagined. It's estimated that your conscious mind, the part of your mind that you're thinking with right now can process about 100 bits of information per second. That's quite a bit, but consider that it's also estimated that your subconscious mind can process about 11 million bits of information per second (Levitin 2015). That's the part of your mind that right now is monitoring your muscle tension, your heart rate, your respiration, and your digestion. And it maintains data about your past experiences as well (Daaisma 2015).

You have been processing tremendous amounts of information every moment, all of your life. That cumulative information is the resource that your inner physician has available, to let you know how you're doing and what you need. You can best access that information by taking quiet time for meditation, deep breathing, and journaling your thoughts and emotions. Then the information is revealed to you in your intuition, your gut feeling, and your hunches. That's why the best doctors will take the time to listen to you, and find out what is going on in your life before diagnosing or recommending treatment.

I highly encourage you to learn to trust your own intuition about what's right for you in terms of your health and your important life decisions. That's how you tune into to your inner physician. Your quiet time is your time for processing and integration of all of the information your brilliant mind has accumulated.

Think of it this way. If you're working on a computer and you're constantly inputting data, and you never hit enter and wait for the output, how much information are you going to get from that computer? None. I think that's one of the ways that we run ourselves and run our own lives...we are constantly receiving input, but we don't give ourselves the time to process.

One of the reasons we don't take the time for self-reflection is that the inner journey can sometimes be daunting. If you have anger you've never dealt with, for example, when you sit down and try to relax you might feel agitated, nervous, or exhausted from the job of resisting your own emotions. Looking at the concentric circles in the inner journey diagram, you can see that if you get past your anger and defenses, you will run into fear. Your mind will get busy at that point, saying "I don't need to do this. I've got more important things to do. I can't be sitting here and doing this. This is ridiculous. People need me, and they expect me to meet their needs." So, you get up and you get busy again. This is called the retreat to the familiar, just doing what you've always done.

So why do something that is so unpleasant at first? Simply because you either work on your emotions or they will work on you. By being courageous enough to make your inner journey and bring your emotions into full conscious awareness, you are potentially preventing numerous types of problems.

As we've discussed, unexpressed and unresolved negative emotions interfere with physical well-being, and also interfere with healthy communication in close relationships. Think of the inner journey as doing some "internal house cleaning." It will enhance your health and your quality of life. It may help you prevent illness and actually contribute to your longevity.

Take time regularly to get calm and quiet and listen to your inner physician. You may get guidance as simple as "Breathe more deeply. Relax more. Have more fun." You may also feel guided to be more of a Goodfinder[1] in your life, practicing gratitude, appreciation, and optimism moment by moment throughout your day (DeFoore 2022).

The Reward For Your Inner Journey

AND THE ULTIMATE REWARD for the inner journey is the connection you make with your core, your original inner child who wants more than anything to love and be loved. The journey through your anger, your fear, and your pain takes you into direct contact with your capacity for great love, joy and well-being.

That's the reward of the inner journey, when you take a little time to listen, to pay attention to your own inner brilliance and then act on that information. When you do that consistently, over time, those barriers of negative emotions start coming down. You're no longer holding the resistance in your body, and your health grows as a result. The more you practice these skills the more proficient your inner physician becomes.

1. https://amzn.to/3DE882u

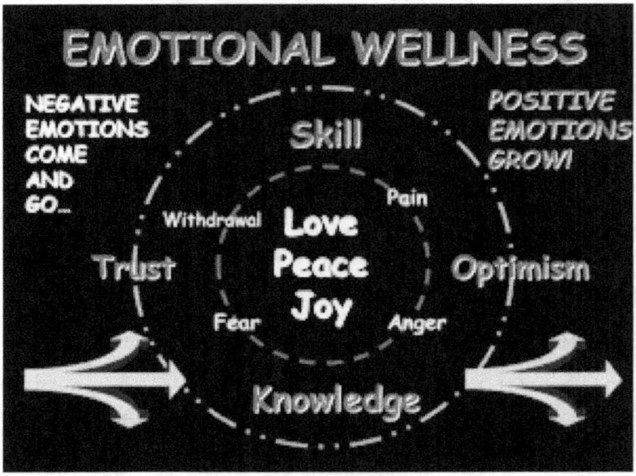

THIS IS A TYPE OF EMOTIONAL upgrade, where you are literally moving to a higher vibrational state of being. All emotion is energy, and all energy is vibrating at different frequencies on an ongoing basis. The higher your vibrational frequency, the healthier, happier, and kinder you will be.

Your knowledge, skills, strength and awareness will be greater as a result of your inner journey. The pain, fear, and anger are still there, but they're transitory. The negative emotions come and go, and the positive emotions grow. This is what it means to be mentally and emotionally healthy.

You're getting ready to adjust to having more positive emotions. Love, joy, enthusiasm, and peace of mind. You were designed to feel that way most of the time.

One of the most positive of all human emotions is exuberance. Most of us as adults don't have a lot of that, if any. But do children have exuberance? Yes. Were we once children? Yes. We have all had exuberance in our life. Where did it go? What happened?

I suggest that what happened to our exuberance is that the buildup of unexpressed, unresolved pain, fear, and anger created a barrier stopping its expression. By practicing the skills we're going to discuss in this book, you will move through those barriers, and gain easier access to your naturally occurring positive emotions, even including exuberance.

Other words to describe these healthier levels of mental and emotional well-being include "wise" and "mature." Do you know someone you would consider to be wise and mature? A lot of times when we think about somebody who's wise and mature, we think about an older person. And yet, have you ever known an older person who was neither wise nor mature? It happens.

And have you ever known a young person who was both wise and mature? That is also very possible, because wisdom and maturity are not specifically tied to chronological age, or even life experience. The good news about this is that wisdom and maturity are accessible to you regardless of your age or stage of life experience.

I would guess that the people that you consider to be wise and mature would also be people who have some ability to deal with their emotions in healthy ways. They most likely experience the full range of emotions, and are able to move through them with some degree of grace and fluidity. Another term that fits here is emotional intelligence, which simply means being intelligent about your emotions, and being intelligent in how you manage and express them.

Chapter Six: The Many Benefits Of Healthy Anger

So what is healthy anger? How could anger be healthy? That term is sort of an oxymoron, like emotional intelligence. Conventionally, we have believed that if you're healthy, you're not angry, and if you're intelligent, you're not emotional.

You're getting a good mental stretch here, to think about being healthy with your anger and intelligent with your emotions.

The main thing to understand about healthy anger is that it is fuel for effective action. When anger is healthy, it doesn't look, sound or feel like anger as we've usually thought of it.

Most people equate anger with aggression, attack, and venting. That is unhealthy anger, and it serves no useful purpose except in extreme life or death circumstances. Even then, if anger takes over, it can interfere with higher brain functions and impair decision making. In sports and combat situations, anger needs to work along with your awareness (emotional intelligence) in order to be helpful and not harmful.

Some examples of healthy anger include the stories of mothers lifting vehicles off of their loved ones (Hill 2003), and *Mothers Against Drunk Drivers* (MADD.org 2023). These are situations in which mothers recognized risk and harm to their children and took powerful, effective action to save them. Their anger was of total benefit, and did no harm to anyone. Walk through this with me...these mothers' deepest emotion for their children was love. The pain of loss was excruciating, and the fear of further loss fueled tremendous anger as a primal, protective emotion.

But these women channeled the powerful energy of those emotions into productive, constructive action.

When we talk about healthy anger, we're entering a completely new territory. Healthy anger is nothing more and nothing less than fuel for powerful and beneficial action.

Here is another example of healthy anger, a more common one we can all relate to: You go out to eat, and your meal arrives. You notice that the fish smells bad. It happens, right? But let's say that you don't want to hurt the waiter's feelings. You don't want to spoil the dinner for others you're with. So, you decide to just pretend. You pick at your meal and spread it around on your plate so it looks like you've eaten something. You then leave the restaurant feeling hungry and not too happy. Or, you get furious and embarrass everyone by being rude to the server. Clearly, neither of these are good choices, but they are actually quite common examples of unhealthy anger.

With healthy anger, you would simply say to the server "Excuse me, this fish is just not right. It doesn't smell right. Could I get something else?" If you say this respectfully, with a pleasant expression, no one will be embarrassed. Usually, you will get a good replacement, and your meal might even be comped.

THE PURPOSE OF ANGER is protection. When you express yourself in this way, you're protecting yourself from spending money on something you don't utilize. And you're protecting yourself from going home feeling bad.

Thinking of these examples of healthy anger expression, you can easily see that there is focus, clarity, energy, and motivated enthusiasm in the communication. These processes are beneficial to your health, increase your intimacy skills, and enhance your overall communication with others.

Let's look at another example. You go to a place of business or retail store. The person behind the counter is on their cell phone, and you can tell it's a personal call. They are ignoring you, and you'd like to get some service. So a healthy anger response would be something like this.

You get around where you are in their field of vision, if possible. In a voice loud enough to be heard, you say "Excuse me, excuse me, miss? Excuse me sir? Hello, can I get some service over here please?" This doesn't look like anger. It doesn't sound like anger, although you might be feeling some. You're not being aggressive, you're being assertive. You're being clear and you've got some energy and enthusiasm in your voice, and ideally a slight smile on your face. This works. Try it.

If these situations of getting poor service trigger a strong anger or rage response in you, that tells you that you need to do some healing of your underlying anger before you will be successful with these healthy anger assertive skills.

Suppressing anger is harmful to our health, and exploding in anger hurts you and your relationships. The healthy expression of anger is good for our health, because you're not going against your values and your good heart.

With healthy anger, you have more flexibility, emotionally, physically, and socially. The person with healthy anger is more socially flexible because she can go anywhere and doesn't have to worry about fearing confrontation. If you're not comfortable with other people's anger or your own, you're going to have to avoid certain social situations.

Emotional flexibility and physical flexibility go hand in hand. Healthy emotion moves throughout your body, and unhealthy emotion gets stuck. If your emotional energy is moving in your body, you're going to be more supple and flexible. If you suppress your anger, you're going to have tension and rigidity in your body, impairing natural functions.

Persistence is the ability to stay with the task to the end. Healthy anger gives us that energy and that ability. With healthy anger, you'll have less stress in your life overall, greater concentration, and more laughter because you're removing the barriers to your health and happiness. As this happens, joy naturally emerges.

You can see how this contributes directly to a greater sense of personal power, a more positive attitude and more self-discipline. Let's look at an application of this to your health and wellness.

Let's say you've just started a new plan for getting healthier, stronger, and more fit overall. You may be motivated by health problems, or just the desire to feel better in your body. So you set out your own plan, or you sign up for a prescribed plan created by others. You're ready to go, and you're feeling good about what you're doing and the outcomes you hope to achieve.

Now, the first week you're probably going to be pretty good on that plan, aren't you? Maybe the second week, maybe even the third. But over time, what do you think happens with most people? Either a slow or sudden slipping back to the old familiar patterns. This of course is very frustrating, and you may be angry at yourself when this happens.

Here is a way to use your healthy anger to be successful in reaching your goals. We will use the challenge of aging, since that is something we all face sooner or later.

Visualize in front of you two images of your future self. One image is of you aging poorly and in declining health. You know that image, because sadly it happens a lot. You know the picture I'm talking about. Loss of mental and physical health and function. It's not where you want to go, but many of us fear that it is inevitable.

And now right beside that image, picture yourself vibrant and healthy in your aging process. See yourself in your mind's eye as alive, alert, awake, and energized. In this image, you are strong, happy, and fit. We know people who are like this, fortunately. Think of the people you know in their 70's, 80's, and beyond, that are doing great. They are your role models.

So, we've got these two pictures of your future self, two possible futures. Use your healthy anger to say "No!" to the first one. Say to yourself, "I am not going there." And use the energy of your healthy anger to say "Yes!" to the second one. "That's me! That's where I'm going!

Then write out a detailed, step-by-step plan for going...get ready for it...in both directions! Why make a plan for going where you don't want to go? So that you'll know when you're heading the wrong way. Your plan for declining health and happiness would include things like, watch lots of tv, spend hours on screen time with social media and gaming, avoid exercise, stay indoors, keep repeating the same thoughts and beliefs without examining them. Allow boredom to dominate. Just let your old habits rule. If this is what you're already doing, then this will be all too easy for you. But there's a trick here.

Easy gets hard. The longer you stay on this self-destructive path, the more tired and sick you will become, until you are sick and tired of your life. This is not what you want for yourself.

Knowing exactly what you're doing that takes you in the direction of unhappiness, illness, and decline will help you change your behavior. If you leave these processes in the unconscious level, you won't even know that you're heading toward a destination you do not want.

Now write out a detailed, step-by-step plan for going in the direction you choose. This means getting regular exercise (outdoors as much as possible), cultivating great friendships, and developing positive practices such as you will find in my book *Goodfinding: A User's Guide to EQ and Your Brilliant Mind*[1] (2022). This means being intentional and focused in your thoughts and actions. Does this sound too hard? It will be, at first, because you will be changing old habits. The good news is that the longer you do it, the easier it becomes.

Here's your takeaway from the two directions: Easy gets hard, and hard gets easy. You get to decide, and decide, and decide again.

When you choose a positive future for yourself, you are transforming your healthy anger into determination and commitment.

I've often heard people comment that they were on track with their diet and exercise program, but then the holidays came along, and they got off track. Or, they were writing in their gratitude journal, then got too busy and haven't restarted their daily practice. The question is not whether you got off track or not, the question is, did you get back on track? If you missed a meal or a shower, you wouldn't say, well I used to eat and shower, but I got off track. This is actually a good analogy, because healthy diet, exercise, and good mental health practices are as important to your well-being as eating and showering.

---

1. *https://amzn.to/3LhxesE*

So, like they say in Alcoholics Anonymous, "Keep coming back." Keep getting back to your practices. Life happens, and you will waver, but don't let that stop you.

You are heading toward a future that you do want, or one that you don't want, all day every day. Take charge of the process and become the master of your own destiny.

Chapter Seven: Healthy Emotional Expression For Release

As we discussed previously, to understand healthy emotional expression we have to distinguish between release and communication.

Let's get back to our example of the late spouse. We're going to look at a totally healthy way of responding.

When I see that she has arrived and she is safe, I don't want to release all of my pent-up emotions on her. I love her. I know it will only hurt her and push her away. It won't do any good. And, I don't want to just hold it inside and make myself miserable.

So let's say that she has come in, and we're looking at each other. I say "It's late. I'm really glad you're okay. I was really worried about you. But I'm kind of upset right now, and I want to sleep and calm down before we talk. I'd like to talk tomorrow when I've got my head straight." That's an important skill to have. When you're both tired and emotional, it's not a good time to try to communicate.

Next morning arrives. First, I'll focus on releasing my pent-up emotions, then I'll do my best to communicate in such a way that will take us toward a solution to the problem.

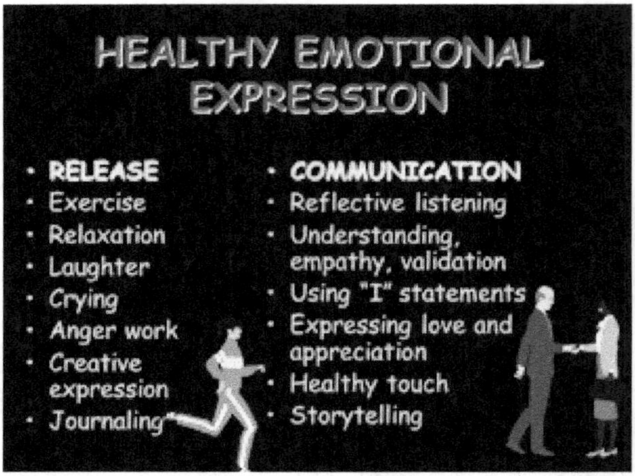

Healthy Emotional Release

THE AGE-OLD SAYINGS of "Count to 10" "Take a breath" and "Take a walk around the block" come from some good awareness. If you can wait a moment, do some deep breathing, and get some exercise, it will give you a chance to activate your higher brain functions. Unhealthy, reactive anger comes from primitive brain functions which can actually shut down the higher brain functions that are activated when you breathe, relax, and move around a bit.

As I prepare to communicate with my partner in our example scenario, it would also be good to do some deep breathing and relaxation. It is impossible to be extremely angry while also being physically relaxed and breathing deeply. Diaphragmatic breathing is an excellent skill to master, and it will benefit you emotionally and physically (Hopper, et. al. 2018).

It would also be helpful to do some anger journaling, as you'll find described on my website AngerManagementResource.com[1]

As I go through the process of relaxing and releasing some of my pent-up emotions, I might even be able to see the humor in some of my reactions. Take a look at some of the worst-case scenarios that have been running through your mind if this was you in this situation. Most of these scenarios never come true, and when you look at them from a detached perspective, you can see how they are a little silly at times.

Laughter is the best medicine. If you can laugh at yourself, that is if you can see your anger as if you were watching it from the outside, it will definitely give you some relief. Taking yourself too seriously when you're angry will never do you any good. To be healthy, anger has to work side by side with love, empathy, and compassion. And if you can sprinkle in a little harmless humor, all the better.

While you're watching this angry part of you from the outside, you'll notice something. It just wants to attack. And if you imagine yourself in our example, it wants to attack the person you love. That's why you don't want your anger running solo. If you let it, it will destroy your relationship and your health.

You realize your anger is there, and you accept it. But you do not let it run the show. It's just not smart enough by itself.

We'll get back to our example of the late spouse in a bit, when we talk about healthy anger in communication.

While you're getting some exercise and practicing deep breathing, let yourself feel the anger, and maybe even growl a little as you push hard on your run, your walk, or your pushups. That's healthy release. Anger is energy, and it needs to come out in healthy ways.

During your releasing process, some tears may come. While releasing the anger, or during deep breathing and relaxation, you may find some sorrow welling up. That's good, and it needs to be released. It will help you to be more clear when you communicate.

---

1. https://www.angermanagementresource.com/anger-management-activities.html#anger-journaling

As human beings, we need to cry as much as we need to laugh. Fortunately, however, we need to laugh a lot more than we need to cry.

We need lots of laughter every day. We don't need lots of crying every day, but there is a time where we do need to cry, isn't there? And what happens if we need to cry and we don't?

If you've had a deep loss and don't know how to cry, or you don't let yourself cry, what happens? The suppression of the emotion can lead to illness, depression, or even anger.

So, we've got laughter and crying right here together, because there is a thin line between joy and sorrow. We've all heard that all our lives, haven't we? Have you ever known anybody who laughs so hard they started crying, or cried so hard they started laughing?

If we know how to go to that place between joy and sorrow, and cross that line, it is a tremendous resource of healing and energy.

One of the skill sets that is very helpful with this is something called anger work, as described in the book *Anger: Deal With It Heal With It Stop It From Killing You*[2] (DeFoore 2004). It's a series of exercises for releasing the built-up energy of toxic anger, such as loud vocal release and physical release like hitting a pillow or mattress with a tennis racket. I know it seems silly, sounds embarrassing, but it's a whole lot better than a heart attack or a failed marriage.

So go ahead and get a little silly and embarrass yourself by throwing a little temper tantrum in the privacy of your bedroom once in a while, to lengthen your life or improve your relationships. It's like going to a dumping ground. Anger work is just a place to get that built up, up negative emotion out in a way that doesn't hurt you or anyone else.

The Power Of Creative Expression

CREATIVITY IS NOTHING more and nothing less than doing something you've never done before. It is also creative to do something you've only done a few times, or doing something you've done many

2. *https://amzn.to/3pybXTv*

timed, but doing it differently. You are being creative when you are charting new territory in your thoughts, emotions, and actions.

In many ways, creativity is a mindset. You can approach your day, your next hour, and each moment in a creative mindset, recognizing that this moment, this hour, this day has never happened before and you can do it with a fresh and energized attitude if you choose.

Many of us think that being creative has to do with producing something that impresses other people. Making great music, painting beautiful art, etc. and presenting it to others is often considered to be creativity, and it is indeed.

But so is the child's fingerpainting mess that she's making in her spilled lunch. The radio built from spare parts found in a junkyard, the graffiti on the railroad car, cooking a meal without following a recipe, or taking a trip without planning ahead are all examples of creative expression. And most of these will receive little or no attention from others.

There are two major stages of the creative process:

1. Your own private process. Regardless of how you are being creative, it can be joyful and uplifting to you to be creative for its own sake, and for your own benefit. This part has nothing to do with other people, and is highly recommended for your health and happiness.
2. Sharing your creative outcomes with others. So you've had a great time writing your song, your poem, or your book. You've really enjoyed your weaving, knitting, sculpting, or garden designing. And you want to share it with others. This changes things a bit, as you know. You feel one way about your project, and when you present it to others, you run into the complex universe of their experience, their opinion, and their capacity for offering positive feedback. This is where many people shut down their creative expression, concluding that they are not

creative because of the response of other people. This is a tragedy, and hopefully reading this will help you to recover your creativity and reignite that spark within you.

3. You keep going, no matter what. Keep writing, dancing, painting, weaving, composing, singing, playing whatever you play. Your creativity belongs to you, and no one else. Other people's opinions, judgments, and criticisms are irrelevant. Don't stop, regardless. Tweak what you're doing, if you want, or try something new. But just keep pursuing your creative expression. It is key to life itself.

It is essential that you claim the value of creativity throughout your life, and give only secondary consideration to stage two listed above.

A lot of people don't get this three-part perspective on creativity. Teachers, for example, have often made the mistake of thinking they are the ones to decide if their students are creative. This is why studies have shown consistently that creative expression declines in some traditional schools (Lynch 2019). Children are naturally creative, whether they are creating messes or something of perceived value. The creative imagination is something to be nurtured and valued, and yet many of us have had this literally programmed out of us.

How common are the beliefs such as "I'm not very creative." "I'm not artistic." "I can't carry a tune." "I don't have a creative bone in my body." These are all mistaken beliefs based on inappropriate negative feedback from others. Everyone is creative, and the forms of creative expression are as individual and unique as our hair, skin, and body types.

So, if you're used to doing things in a certain way, change it up a little bit. That's creative. Try your hand at something that is fun for you. Forget whether it's "any good" or not, just have fun with it. And if it's fun, keep doing it. Do it for its own sake, and only share it with people if you think they will be positive and encouraging. You're not trying to win any prizes, you're just going for the emotional benefit of creative expression.

If you choose to take an art class, music lesson, or any other type of instruction on your chosen form of creativity, look for instructors that are positive and supportive. Criticism stifles creativity, and there is no place for it in this type of learning. And again, consider just doing it on your own, or learn from a book or video. It's just for you.

And while we're on the subject of creativity, I want to mention the study called the Nun Study, which was done with a group of nuns to determine some of the lifestyle variables that contributed to the occurrence of Alzheimer's. This study indicated that two lifestyle variables predicted the non-occurrence of Alzheimer's in this group of nuns that were studied (Snowdon 2002). One was creative expression. The nuns who were more creative in their expression were the least likely to get Alzheimer's. And the other lifestyle variable that contributed to healthy brains was positive emotional expression.

So expressing positive emotions and expressing yourself creatively could be one of the best things you can do to prevent the occurrence of Alzheimer's. It's so easy to just do what you've always done. It's much easier to feel and express negative emotion than it is to go into positive. It takes no effort to be afraid. Live in this world, go out on the freeway, read the news, and guess what? You're afraid.

It also takes no effort to be angry. Move around in this world, bump into a few things, and no problem, you're angry. It requires no effort to be sad, because loss is a natural and inevitable part of life.

But is it that easy to feel love, an overflowing feeling of joy, excitement, and enthusiasm? No, it's not. It requires some effort, and some creativity. If you want good news to make you feel better, you're going to have to search for it, and that searching, that effort, is beneficial.

In order to feel good and raise your energy level and your joy, happiness, and health, you're going to have to make some effort to look for reasons to feel good. That effort is going to be creative. That's going to make your brain work better, and may reduce the likelihood of you getting Alzheimer's according to this one research program, as well as others (Shelley 2019). To increase your skills for feeling and expressing positive emotions, become a Goodfinder[3] (DeFoore 2022).

Journaling For Healthy Emotional Expression

JOURNALING IS SIMPLY a process of taking the very busy activity in our mind and putting it down on paper. You know the thoughts that sometimes keep you up at night and then just go on and on when we're worried about something? Have you ever noticed how that goes in loops? It's not very interesting. It's like the same thoughts over and over and over, and it loops around. When you write it down on a piece of paper, you're not going to write in loops and circles. You're going to stretch out the loops.

Writing down your thoughts is going to help you to sort them out and organize them, and you'll be able to observe your own thought processes much easier if you write them down than if you're just thinking them. So, it can be a way of getting back to sleep when your mind is keeping you awake, and also a way of understanding yourself better.

Dr. James Pennebaker's research with writing about emotional experiences has demonstrated that the "languaging" process of journaling is beneficial in resolving trauma and reducing stress. His studies further indicate that writing about traumatic experiences actually leads to a reduction in medical visits among the subjects who participated in his research (2016).

Learn more about journaling processes for anger release, emotional healing, and developing a positive mindset in this article on AngerManagementResource.com[4].

---

3. https://amzn.to/3LhxesE

4. https://www.angermanagementresource.com/anger-management-activities.html

Chapter Eight: Communicating Emotions In Healthy Ways

If you're talking and nobody's really listening, are you communicating? Clearly, you are not communicating unless someone is listening to you. As obvious as this is, it is surprising how many people think that talking is communicating. A parent lecturing on and on to her child, for example, is not communicating, for a number of reasons. One is that children's attention span is fairly short, they are more nonverbal than verbal in the early years, and the human mind tunes out unwanted noise quite effectively.

If you're feeling a strong emotion, you want to communicate. You don't just want to talk, vent, or lecture. Think of our example. If you're the partner who was at home waiting, you will want to vent perhaps, but any benefit from that is only short-term. Mostly, you will want to communicate. Talking when nobody's listening is a waste of time and energy, and will only lead to greater frustration and discord.

Authentic communication is actually a fairly subtle and sophisticated process. There is a speaker, and a listener or listeners. Let's look at both parts of this equation.

The Speaker

IF YOU WANT PEOPLE to listen to you, you need to know something about who they are, what their interests are, what mood they might be in, and the relevance of what you want to say. This requires empathy and knowledge on your part as the speaker, not just talking away because something happens to pop into your mind, or emotionally venting your feelings to reduce the buildup of pressure inside.

Here are some suggestions for healthy communication, and speaking in such a way that will not lead to conflict (the following ten suggestions are excerpted from *Goodfinding: A User's Guide to EQ and Your Brilliant Mind* (2022):

- Make queries about others' content. To show your genuine interest, you will want to ask questions about what your partner is saying, such as, "I'm curious about how that happened. Tell me more about that," or "What's that like for you?"
- Make positive statements about others' interests and accomplishments. When it feels appropriate, make statements such as "I am so impressed that you're doing that," "I admire your courage and self-confidence in taking that on," and "I like what you're doing in your (artwork, music, volunteering, work, etc.)."
- Keep all statements as positive as possible. While it may seem like an easy thing to share the latest negative news story or tell others about your latest trauma, illness, or frustration, this will not build the types of relationships you will enjoy. Try to take the high road at every opportunity and share positive, uplifting, fun, or funny stories and viewpoints.
- Offer your own stories and experiences. Only after focusing for a while on your partner's stories and content should you offer your own input that relates to hers or his. You keep the focus strong on the other's content so that you're making it clear that you're interested in what that person is offering, not just looking for a way to shift the focus to you. When you bring in your own content, keep it brief, or at least balanced in terms of time.

- Read your partners' interest levels from their nonverbal signals. While speaking, read your listeners' interest levels in what you're saying by looking at their eyes, which will tell you how engaged they are. If they don't seem interested or seem too distracted to listen to what you're saying, wrap it up quickly and shift the focus back to them.
- Keep your statements to two or three at a time. When speaking to another, don't make more than a few statements before pausing for the other to respond. If you are in a close, comfortable relationship and it appears that the other is genuinely interested in what you're saying, you can make as many as five or six statements before pausing or sometimes tell an even longer story.
- Use qualifying statements before offering strong opinions. Before offering your opinions, especially strong declarations or statements that may challenge your partner, preface those opinions with qualifying phrases such as "as far as I can tell," "it seems to me that," "I'm not completely sure, but" and "in my experience." This is important because while you may be very sure of what you're saying, your partner may have very different viewpoints. If you speak with too much certainty without these qualifiers, she or he may feel that you're claiming some type of authority on the topic that you don't rightfully have.
- Avoid offering unsolicited advice, correction, and criticism. The independence and autonomy of the human spirit is such that most people do not enjoy or benefit from unsolicited advice or correction. Overt criticism will almost always be rejected. Think of the positive psychology approach of building on strengths instead of pointing out weaknesses or shortcomings. It works better.

- Avoid venting or unloading. While some people believe that venting to a friend or family member is an acceptable form of conversation, it is in fact much more detrimental than helpful. Think about the receiver of the venting for a moment. Have you ever looked forward to a conversation because you knew someone wanted to vent or unload? Most likely not. The person doing the venting might feel better temporarily while unloading, but the benefit won't last. This is just another form of complaining, which is a dysfunctional method of communication. Choose solution-based problem-solving, placing the greatest emphasis on the solutions, and you will fare much better, as will your relationships.

- Practice nonattachment to your partner's agreement or disagreement. Try not to mind too much whether others agree or disagree with what you're saying. This makes for a much more relaxed experience for everyone. The purpose of conversation and communication is not to convince or persuade anyone of anything. It is to build connections and community.

Learn and practice all of the steps to healthy communication during stressful or conflictual conversations in a step-by-step guide on AngerManagementResource.com[1] (DeFoore 2007). This includes many guidelines for the speaker, including the use of "I" statements and taking personal responsibility for emotional content.

The Listener

ONE OF THE BEST WAYS to keep your listener engaged is to be a good listener yourself. As mentioned above, ask questions about the other person's interests or concerns, and practice reflective listening so that they know for sure that they have been heard.

1. https://www.angermanagementresource.com/bad-relationships.html#communication-skills

Reflective listening is an extremely powerful tool for these important purposes:

- To maintain a connection with your communication partner, especially during times of disagreement, conflict, or misunderstanding.
- To let your partner know you care about them as a person, and you're interested in their viewpoint whether you agree or not.
- To open the doorway to empathy and compassion in your relationship.
- To prevent the unconscious pattern of preparing your response while the other person is talking, instead of giving them your full attention.
- To prevent the tit-for-tat back and forth debate style of conversation that leads to conflict and stressful relationships.

The methodology of reflective listening is as follows:

- Pay attention to the exact words your partner is using, especially words with strong emotional content.
- When you've heard them out and they are pausing for your response, make one of these lead-in statements, followed by your best effort to repeat what they have said:
    - What I hear you saying is...
    - If I'm understanding you correctly, you're saying...
    - Let me see if I'm understanding you. You're saying...
    - I want to make sure I understand what you're saying. It seems to me that you're saying...
    - Help me understand. What I hear you saying is...
- Then give them a chance to correct or elaborate. Hold your opinions and responses at bay during this part of the process. If they say, "Yes, that's it" or "Exactly!" Then you can move on with the conversation. If they elaborate, however, repeat the

above process of listening and reflecting.

- For this to work, you have to genuinely care about your partner and your relationship with them. If you don't, or if you're angry, frustrated, or dominated by your critical mind, it's best not to try this technique. Your negative feelings will come through, and your reflective listening skills will not work. Practice loving kindness meditation[2] (Seppala 2021) before communicating if needed, and this will help you move into a compassionate mindset.

Reflective listening clarifies what the other person has said so that they feel heard, but it doesn't stop there. Once your partner feels heard, you want to express empathy and validation for their feelings and viewpoint, whether you agree with them or not.

You say something like "When I put myself in your shoes, I think I can understand where you're coming from." Empathy is key to good communication. An interesting little piece of research about empathy is, it was found in the book *Emotional Intelligence*[3] (Goleman 2020). They found that people who were identified as abusers were people who lacked empathy skills. The abuser tells himself a lie about the victim, in order to justify the abuse.

Reflective listening and empathy skills unlock this destructive pattern, allowing healthy connections and better decision making.

Many times, working with couples, I find that they're both really good people with good hearts, they love each other. And yet because of their inability to communicate, they think that they don't like each other and that the other person's not such a good person. But that's often a misperception. I can see very clearly that they're both good people and

---

2. https://ggia.berkeley.edu/practice/loving_kindness_meditation

3. *https://www.amazon.com/Emotional-Intelligence-Matter-More-Than/dp/055338371X/ref=tmm_pap_swatch_0?_encoding=UTF8&qid=1689686721&sr=8-1*

want the same thing. They're communication style just turns into a battle without them knowing why.

The basic communication skills described above create a bridge where people can begin to see who the other person really is, not just who they think they are.

Instead of really perceiving what's going on with the victim, the abuser tells himself it doesn't hurt her. He makes up stories that she wants it, or had it coming. So, in empathy, what we do is we get the truth of what's going on with the other person, which allows compassion and encourages better choices.

Let's go back to our example of the couple where the partner is late.

He doesn't have any good excuses, but he attempts to explain anyway. He says "I just lost track of time. I figured I could get here in time, but I got distracted. You know how I am."

You're not quite ready to divorce him over this, so you're looking for a way to keep the connection going, even though you're upset.

Here are some things you might say:

- I hear you saying you lost track of time, and got distracted.
- I can understand how that could happen. It's happened to me.
- I know you have problems with managing your focus, and getting things done on time. I know that's hard for you.
- I've also noticed that if something is really important to you, you will stay focused and get the job done, every time, and you will be on time.
- I want to be that important to you. I want our relationship to matter that much to you, that you will be a reliable partner to me and do what you say you're going to do.

This allows you to express your feelings, but without attack or venting. With this type of communication, you're not harming the relationship, and you may actually help it. The rest is up to your partner.

Expressing Emotions Through Healthy Touch

WE ALL NEED HEALTHY touch. Touch starvation is a very real problem for many people, and for many different reasons (Sharkey 2021).

If you're not getting enough touch in your life, consider the possibility of getting regular massage, or attending a cuddle party[4], until you are able to get into a relationship where you're getting plenty of touch. You can also get a pet, as it has been shown that petting animals helps to fulfill needs for safe, healthy touch.

Regular, healthy touch is essential to our mental, emotional, and physical health, and there is no substitute. Symptoms of touch starvation include depression, anxiety, and sleep problems. And healthy touch has actually been shown to boost immune function. This is just too important to ignore or overlook.

Some people have a lot of fear around touch because of all of the issues around inappropriate touch and sexual violation. But you're not going to get in trouble for putting your hand on your spouse's shoulder, back, or arm. And it's probably okay holding hands a little more often, and hugging your friends.

There's a whole lot of safe touch available if we look for it, and we need it.

The Power Of Storytelling

YOU NEED TO KNOW AND tell your own story. If your friends and loved ones don't know your story, they don't know you. Of course you won't tell it all at one time, but a healthy relationship is one in which both people share segments of their life story periodically throughout the relationship.

---

4. https://cuddleparty.com/

You're the main character of your story, and at this point you can claim a little bit of authorship of your story going forward. You have a lot of creative choice in how your continuing story unfolds.

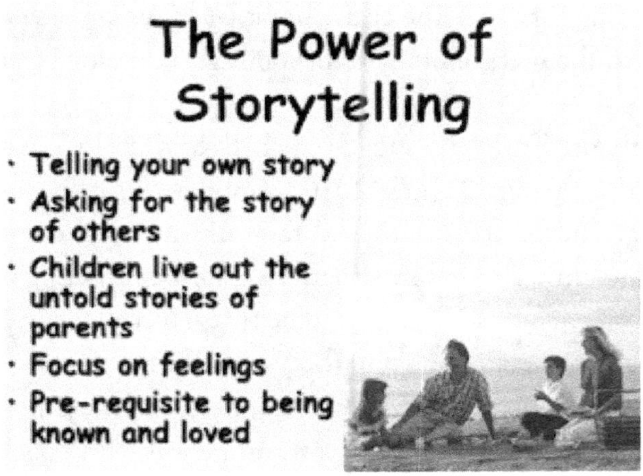

WE ALSO NEED TO ASK for the stories of others. Every one of us is living out a story, and we need to be aware of it. Imagine the timeline of your life story. You're here in the present, and you look back at your birth, which is where your story began. Look at the major events that made you who you are today and write them down. Write about what you learned from these major events, and share these insights with others when appropriate.

Then look at where you want your story to go from here. That's where you can use the visioning process we referred to earlier. Simply look at the two pictures of your future life, and decide which direction you choose.

There's a book called *Write It Down, Make It Happen*[5] (Klauser 2001). It's an excellent book that takes the idea of visioning and puts it into the writing-down process, which is a way of moving forward in the creation of your story from this point forward.

As children, we didn't have a lot of authorship or authority in our story. Now as adults, we do. Now we can become conscious creators of our story going forward. The entire book *Goodfinding*[6] (DeFoore 2022) is devoted to the methodology of becoming a conscious creator in your life.

Psychologist Karl Jung suggested that children live out the untold stories of their parents (Jung 2010), emphasizing the importance of storytelling. This is not a hard and fast rule, as it varies tremendously from child to child and family situations. In my counseling practice, and in my personal life, I have found it to be true in certain ways.

As a personal example, my father was a World War II veteran who fought in the Pacific. During his service, he took lives and saw beloved comrades killed. Then he came back from the war with unacknowledged PTSD, married my mom, and six years later I was born into the aftermath of his WWII experience.

In those days, veterans didn't talk about the war, right? He got no therapy or treatment for his PTSD. He was supposed to just go on with life as if those 4 years of unimaginable trauma had not occurred. So, the trauma was all stored inside. He kept his untold stories inside him, but I saw and felt those stories through his eyes, his interactions, and his reactions.

Think about this for a moment. In communication studies, it has been found that 93% of communication is non-verbal (Mehrabian 2007). So, the actual verbal telling of the story is only 7% of communication. Dad told his war stories non-verbally the whole time I

---

5. *https://www.amazon.com/Write-Down-Make-Happen-Knowing/dp/0684850028/ref=tmm_pap_swatch_0?_encoding=UTF8&qid=1689630229&sr=8-1*

6. *https://amzn.to/3LhxesE*

was growing up. And since children begin their lives like sponges soaking up virtually everything, I soaked it up.

Then I realized in my thirties that I had been having nightmares about being at war off and on my whole life. They were so familiar to me that I didn't think anything about it until I was in graduate school studying psychology, and realized that recurring dreams about being at war may not be normal.

So I asked my dad to tell me about the war. He refused, saying that those memories are locked away forever. Then in the next few years he had some experiences of his own that helped him understand how the stories needed to be told, and he began by writing them down. Then he began speaking the stories out loud to me and my brothers.

My nightmares stopped almost immediately. I had been unconsciously living out his untold stories in my dreams. As he got more comfortable talking about the war, he also was more able to talk about his childhood experiences. I remember listening to him, and occasionally having the thought, "So that's why I've always felt that way." I felt something that I had been carrying moving out of me and going back to him. It was healing for him and for me. My brothers had their own experiences with this, none of us exactly the same.

So, look deeply into the important and significant aspects of your story, and tell them to your loved ones. It will help them to know you better, and it may help them in ways you don't fully realize. You may think you're protecting your partner and children by not telling them about any past trauma you've experienced, but you're actually not protecting them at all. They've been "hearing" your untold story through your nonverbal behavior all along.

Focus on the feelings when you're telling your stories. Don't bore them with irrelevant facts and commentary. It is the emotions that make a story real. If you don't fully understand your own story, you don't know yourself. If others don't know your story, they don't know you.

The stories we remember are the ones with the most powerful emotions, whether positive or negative. We don't remember or care about those days where nothing happened, the boring days. It's the powerful ones we recall, the best and the worst of times.

Think of your story as a storehouse, a treasure trove of meaning and value just waiting for your discovery and revelation.

Learn more about your personal mythology and storytelling in *Personal Mythology: Using Ritual, Dreams, and Imagination to Discover Your Inner Story*[7], by Feinstein and Kripper (2009).

---

7. *https://www.amazon.com/Personal-Mythology-Ritual-Imagination-Discover/dp/160415036X/ref=sr_1_1?crid=7ULBJNYDDC6P&keywords=personal+mythology+stanley+krippner&qid=1689686213&sprefix=personal+mythology%2Caps%2C279&sr=8-1*

Chapter Nine: Skills To Take With You

While there are skills mentioned throughout this book, we will cover a summary overview of some basics that are essential for healing anger and depression and becoming the person you choose to be.

- Take responsibility, but don't take blame. There's a big difference. Responsibility gives you the ability to respond. If you're blamed, then you are the bad guy, and all you can do is feel guilty. If you take responsibility, then you have a choice about what you can do.
- Place responsibility, not blame. Remember how I said the angry person is blaming, putting the power out there on the other person or situation? Recognize that a person is behaving in a way that you don't like, and acknowledge that they are responsible for that behavior. But don't blame them for how you feel about it. Your feelings are your responsibility. Do you see the difference there? You're upset. You can't sleep at night because your boss, for example, is giving you a really hard time. Now, is your boss keeping you up at night? No, it's your thoughts and feelings. It's how you're dealing with the situation that's keeping you up at night. Now, that's a hard distinction to make, but extremely important. If you don't want to be a victim of this world and everybody in it, this is a distinction you have to make. Other people are responsible for their behavior, but they are not at fault for how you feel.
- Express your love and appreciation. If you take nothing else

with you today but that, then take that. Express your love and appreciation. Think about the love that you feel for the people that are in this world and in your life. Write it down and tell them about it.

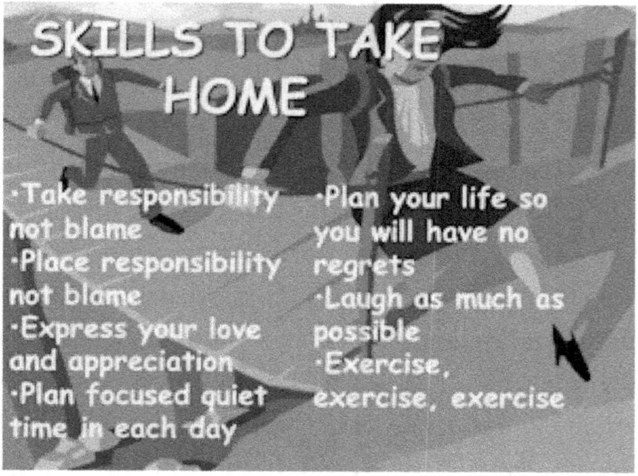

And show them in as many different ways as you can, not just in the words. Shared activities are one of the greatest expressions of love. Let's say you have an adolescent son or daughter or friend or niece or nephew or someone who is doing something that you cannot relate to and don't like. Go and do it with them. If that's not an expression of love, I don't know what is. Doing something you don't like to do and are not interested in, simply because you care about that person. You might get some funny looks when you do this. If it's an adolescent, for example, they might think "What are you doing here? You hate this stuff." And with your actions you are saying "Yeah, but I love you. I want to hang out with you and see what's interesting to you. Help me understand this." Keeping the judgment out of it, and be curious about what lights them up inside.

- Plan focused quiet time in each day. Again, that's where you listen to your own wisdom, the cumulative life experience in your body/mind. You have a brilliant mind, but it speaks to you softly, and if you don't get quiet, you won't hear it. One of the things you may have noticed is, if we don't listen to the quiet voice inside saying "Hey, something doesn't quite feel right here in my gut or in my chest." You think it's not a big deal. Then the voice gets a little louder. "Hey, this is not too cool. This is not feeling good." Ignore that, and the next voice may be a scream and it may be your own. Meaning, if we don't get the early warning signs, then our body is going to grab us and demand our attention through illness. I really believe that if we can learn to listen to all of the subtle indicators of what's going on and respond intelligently and appropriately, we don't have to be as unhealthy and as sick as we often are.

- Plan your life so that you will have no regrets. If you were at the end of your life and someone said, looking back over your life, what would you do differently? What would you say? Most people say, I would spend more time with my family and loved ones. I'd relax more, play more. What would you have to do from this day to the end of your life so that you could say, I wouldn't change a thing?
- Write it down, make it happen. Laugh as much as possible, and exercise, exercise, exercise.

TO LEARN MORE, AND to further your emotional healing and joyful well-being, check out Dr. DeFoore's other books online.

Amazon Author Page[1]

Audiobooks Listing[2]

---

1. https://www.amazon.com/stores/William-G.-DeFoore/author/B004S1PXMC?ref=ap_rdr&store_ref=ap_rdr&isDramIntegrated=true&shoppingPortalEnabled=true
2. https://www.scribd.com/author/364694852/William-G-DeFoore

Inner Child Ebook Series[3]

3. https://www.kobo.com/us/en/series/inner-child-series

References

Healing Anger and Depression

Barkley, S. (2022). What Does It Mean to be Touch Starved? Psychcentral.com. https://psychcentral.com/health/ways-to-self-soothe-when-starved-for-touch#importance

DeFoore, W. (2004). Anger Deal With It Heal With It Stop It From Killing You. Health Communications, Inc.

DeFoore, W. (2007). Conflict resolution communication tools. Angermanagementresource.com.
https://www.angermanagementresource.com/
bad-relationships.html#communication-skills

DeFoore, W. (2007). Getting Your Anger Out On Paper. Angermanagementresource.com.
https://www.angermanagementresource.com/anger-management-activities.html#anger-journaling

DeFoore, W. (2022). Goodfinding: A User's Guide to EQ and Your Brilliant Mind. Balboa Press.

Digma.com. Frederick's Experiment. https://www.digma.com/digma-images/video-scripts/fredericks_experiment.pdf
https://digma.com/fredericks-experiment/?video=play

Draaisma, D. (2015). Forgetting: Myths, Perils and Compensations. Yale University Press

Goleman, D. (2020). Emotional Intelligence 25th Anniversary Edition. Bloomsbury Publishing.

Groopman, J. (2001). Second Opinions: Eight Clinical Dramas of Decision Making on the Front Lines of Medicine. Penguin Books

Hill, D. (2003). Green with Anger. Theguardian.com. https://www.theguardian.com/film/2003/jul/17/comment.features

Hopper S., Murray S., Ferrara L., & Singleton J. (2018). "Effectiveness of diaphragmatic breathing on physiological and psychological stress in adults: a quantitative systematic review protocol". JBI Database of Systematic Reviews and Implementation Reports.

Jung, K. (2010). Dreams. Princeton University Press.

Kensinger EA. (2009). Remembering the Details: Effects of Emotion. Emot Rev. 2009;1(2):99-113. doi: https://journals.sagepub.com/doi/10.1177/1754073908100432

Klauser, H. (2001). Write It Down, Make It Happen: Knowing What You Want And Getting It. Fireside Books.

Feinstein, D. (2009) Personal Mythology: Using Ritual, Dreams, and Imagination to Discover Your Inner Story. Energy Psychology Press.

Lipton, B. (2016). The Biology of Belief. 10th Anniversary Edition: Unleashing the Power of Consciousness, Matter & Miracles. Hay House Inc.

Levitin, D. (2015). Why It's So Hard To Pay Attention, Explained By Science. https://www.fastcompany.com/3051417/why-its-so-hard-to-pay-attention-explained-by-science

Lynch, M. (2019). Kids Are Born Creative Geniuses But The Education System Destroys Imagination. TheEdvocate.com. https://www.theedadvocate.org/kids-are-born-creative-geniuses-but-the-education-system-destroys-imagination/#google_vignette

M.A.D.D. (2023). Mothers Against Drunk Driving. MADD.org. https://madd.org/

Mehrabian, A. (2007). Nonverbal Behavior. Routledge

Pennebaker, J., Smythe, J. (2016). Opening Up by Writing It Down: How Expressive Writing Improves Health and Eases Emotional Pain (3rd ed.). The Guilford Press

Pietrangelo, A. (2019). The Effects of Depression in Your Body. Healthline.com. https://www.healthline.com/health/depression/effects-on-body

Seppala, E. (2021). Loving kindness meditation. Ggia.berkeley.edu. https://ggia.berkeley.edu/practice/loving_kindness_meditation

Sharkey, L. (2021). What Does It Mean To Be Touch Starved? Healthline.com https://www.healthline.com/health/touch-starved

Shelley, (2019) Can Engaging in Art Projects Prevent Alzheimer's? HeritageSeniorCommunities.com. https://www.heritageseniorcommunities.com/can-engaging-in-art-projects-prevent-alzheimers/

Snowdon, D. (2002). Aging with Grace: What the Nun Study Teaches Us About Leading Longer, Healthier, and More Meaningful Lives. Bantam

Sullins, E. (1991). Emotional Contagion Revisited: Effects of Social Comparison and Expressive Style on Mood Convergence. Personality and Social Psychology Bulletin, 17(2), 166–174. https://doi.org/10.1177/0146167291017002008

Also by William DeFoore

Healing Anger
Love, Anger And Forgiveness
Healing Anger And Depression
Anger Management Techniques

Inner Child Series
Nurturing Your Inner Child
Your New Inner Child For Men
Your New Inner Child For Women
Serai: Bringing The Children Home
Ocean Child
Your Inner Child: A Complete Guide to Joy & Healing

Watch for more at https://www.goodfinding.com/.

About the Author

William G. DeFoore, Ph.D. is an author, counselor, coach and speaker who focuses on the power and importance of positive mental focus and emotional intelligence. With 43 years of professional experience, William is author/co-author of five books and 18 audiobooks, many of which focus on the topic of emotional intelligence and emotional wellness. His books and audio programs provide a fresh and practical approach to understanding, healing and expressing emotions in healthy, productive ways so that it becomes an empowering energy fueling productive action and positive communication. His approach fosters the development of emotional integration and emotional intelligence for the purpose of forming and maintaining strong, loving connections with yourself and others.

Read more at https://www.goodfinding.com/.

www.ingramcontent.com/pod-product-compliance
Lightning Source LLC
LaVergne TN
LVHW022312200926
848481LV00004B/1297